AMELIA EARHART

BOOK FOR CURIOUS KIDS

Discover the Life and Adventures of the Pioneering Pilot

MARK LYLANI

MARK LYLANI

TABLE OF CONTENTS

TABLE OF CONTENTS

INTRODUCTION

Who was Amelia Earhart, and what made her such an enduring figure in the history of flight? How did she face challenges, break barriers, and set records that inspired generations of aviators to come? Join us on an exhilarating journey through the life and legacy of Amelia Earhart, a woman whose name became synonymous with courage, determination, and the spirit of adventure.

In this book, we'll uncover the captivating story of Amelia's adventurous beginnings, her groundbreaking achievements in aviation, and the enduring mystery surrounding her disappearance. From her early days of dreaming about flight to her historic flights across continents, Amelia's life is a testament to the power of perseverance and the pursuit of dreams.

Come along as we explore the mysteries, the triumphs, and the lasting legacy of "Lady Lindy," a trailblazer who continues to inspire us to reach for new horizons.

Adventurous Beginnings

Amelia Mary Earhart's story began on July 24, 1897, in Atchison, Kansas, where she was born in a grand house that once belonged to her influential grandfather. She was the second child in her family, with a younger sister named Grace. Before Amelia was born, her parents had experienced the loss of a baby.

Amelia's family was quite extraordinary. Her grandfather, a former judge and respected figure in the community, initially had doubts about her parents' marriage and was not impressed by her father's career as a lawyer.

Amelia was given her name in honor of her grandmothers, Amelia Josephine Harres and Mary Wells Patton, continuing a cherished family tradition. From a young age, Amelia showed leadership qualities, with her sister Grace often following her lead. They had affectionate nicknames—Amelia was called "Meeley" or "Millie," and Grace was known as "Pidge."

Amelia and Grace had an unconventional upbringing. Their mother, Amy, believed in raising her daughters to be strong and independent, challenging the typical expectations for young girls. While most girls in their neighborhood wore dresses, Amelia preferred comfortable bloomers, much to her grandmother's disapproval.

Amelia's early years were filled with adventure and a sense of independence, which laid the groundwork for her extraordinary life. Her family's teachings instilled in her strength and bravery, qualities that would later define her as one of the world's most renowned aviators.

These early experiences shaped Amelia into the fearless and determined woman who would go on to inspire people worldwide.

Discovering the World

Amelia and her sister Grace were two adventurous girls growing up in the early 1900s, a time when the world was just beginning to discover the wonders of flight.

Each day, Amelia and Pidge would rush out of their house, eager to explore their neighborhood. They climbed trees, went on rat-hunting expeditions (with a rifle just for fun!), and zoomed downhill on their sleds, feeling the wind against their faces.

Amelia was different from most girls of her time. She loved the outdoors and didn't mind getting a little dirty. During their adventures, she busily collected worms, moths, and katydids and even once caught a tree toad.

In 1904, Amelia's uncle helped her build something special—a homemade ramp that resembled a roller coaster she had seen in St. Louis. Placed on the roof of their family's toolshed, Amelia bravely climbed onto a wooden box and slid down the ramp. The box broke, and Amelia tumbled out with a bruised lip and torn dress. But instead of crying, she laughed and exclaimed, "Oh, Pidge, it's just like flying!"

When Amelia turned ten, her family moved to Des Moines, Iowa, where her dad worked for the Rock Island Railroad. It was at the Iowa State Fair in Des Moines that Amelia saw her first airplane. Excitedly, her dad suggested they take a ride, but when Amelia saw the rickety-looking plane made of rusty wire and wood, she wasn't too keen. Instead, she asked to go back to the merry-go-round!

Little did Amelia know that her feelings about the biplane would change over the years. Despite finding it boring as a child, she would eventually become one of the most famous pilots in the world! Even from a young age, Amelia's spirit of adventure and her love for the thrill of flying were beginning to grow.

Amelia's childhood experiences and early encounters with airplanes laid the foundation for her future. As she grew older, her passion for flying would lead her to become a trailblazing aviator and an inspiration to generations.

School and Sisterhood

After Amelia's family moved to Des Moines for her father's new job, Amelia and her sister Grace, who now preferred to be called by her middle name Muriel, stayed back in Atchison with their grandparents. While their parents settled into their new home, the girls received their education at home, taught by their mother and a governess.

During this time, Amelia discovered her love for reading. She would lose herself in books, spending hours in the large family library, exploring far-off lands and exciting adventures through the pages of her books. Amelia's curiosity about the world grew with each story she read.

In 1909, after two years apart, the Earhart family reunited in Des Moines. Amelia was now twelve years old and ready to attend public school for the very first time. She entered the seventh grade with excitement and a thirst for knowledge.

Amelia and Muriel's bond as sisters grew stronger during these years. They shared stories, dreams, and adventures together, even as they adapted to a new school and a new city. Amelia's passion for learning continued to shine as she embraced new experiences and challenges.

Facing Challenges

Life became difficult for Amelia and her family as they faced financial troubles and personal challenges. Amelia's father, Edwin, struggled with alcoholism, which caused problems at home.

In 1914, Edwin had to stop working due to his drinking, and despite efforts to get help, he never returned to his job. To make things worse, Amelia's grandmother, Amelia Otis, passed away suddenly, leaving behind money for the family. However, because of Edwin's alcoholism, Amelia's share of the inheritance was put into a trust to protect it.

The family had to sell their house and everything inside it, which was a heartbreaking moment for Amelia. She felt like it was the end of her childhood.

In 1915, Edwin found work in St. Paul, Minnesota, and Amelia started attending Central High School as a junior. But soon, Edwin's job situation changed again, and the family faced more uncertainties. They moved to Chicago, where Amelia struggled to find a school that met her high standards for education.

Despite these challenges, Amelia was determined to pursue her dreams. She graduated from Hyde Park High School in 1916. Throughout her difficult childhood, Amelia never stopped dreaming of a successful career. She collected newspaper clippings about women who succeeded in fields usually dominated by men, like film direction, law, and engineering.

During a visit to Toronto in 1917, Amelia was deeply moved by the wounded soldiers returning from World War I. She trained as a nurse's aide and worked at a military hospital, where she heard stories from pilots that sparked her interest in flying.

Amelia's early years were filled with struggles, but they also fueled her determination to achieve great things.

MARK LYLANI

Conquering Adversity

During Amelia Earhart's time as a nurse's aide at the Spadina Military Hospital in Toronto, a serious flu called the Spanish flu swept through the city in 1918. Amelia worked tirelessly, even taking night shifts to care for the sick soldiers.

Unfortunately, Amelia herself caught the flu and became very ill. She developed pneumonia and a condition called maxillary sinusitis, which caused intense pain and pressure around her eye and a lot of mucus in her nose and throat. Amelia had to stay in the hospital for about two months, enduring painful treatments to try to clear the infection from her sinus.

After she was discharged from the hospital in December 1918, Amelia's recovery took almost a year. She went to live with her sister in Northampton, Massachusetts, where she spent her time reading poetry, learning to play the banjo, and studying mechanics. Despite the setbacks caused by her illness, Amelia remained determined and curious, finding ways to keep her mind active and engaged.

Unfortunately, chronic sinusitis continued to bother Amelia, affecting her ability to fly and engage in activities. Sometimes, she had to wear a bandage on her cheek to cover a small drainage tube, even when she was on the airfield.

Amelia's struggle with illness was a challenging chapter in her life, but she didn't let it stop her from pursuing her dreams. Her time recovering allowed her to explore new interests and skills, setting the stage for her future achievements in aviation.

First Flights

Amelia Earhart's fascination with flying began to soar in the early 1920s, marking the start of her extraordinary journey into the skies.

In 1920, while at Columbia University, Amelia embarked on a daring adventure by climbing to the top of the library dome and exploring hidden tunnels. This exhilarating experience sparked her sense of adventure.

Not long after, Amelia attended an air fair in Toronto with a friend. The excitement and thrill of the flying exhibition captured her imagination. She watched in awe as a World

War I ace performed daring maneuvers in the sky. Little did Amelia know that day would leave a lasting impression on her.

By 1919, Amelia was preparing to attend Smith College but changed her plans to study medical subjects and other programs at Columbia University. However, she later left to be with her parents in California.

Amelia's life changed forever on December 28, 1920, when she attended an aerial meet with her father in Long Beach, California. Inspired and curious, Amelia booked her first passenger flight for the following day. For $10, she soared through the skies with Frank Hawks, a famous air racer. The moment she lifted off the ground, Amelia knew she had found her passion—flying.

The spark ignited; Amelia sought out flying lessons and found Neta Snook, a pioneering female aviator, to be her instructor. Working various jobs to save money, Amelia was determined to pursue her dream of flying. On January 3, 1921, at Kinner Field, Amelia took her first flying lesson in a Curtiss JN-4 "Canuck," traveling four miles by foot and bus just to reach the airfield.

Against her mother's reservations, Amelia invested in her own plane—a bright yellow Kinner Airster she lovingly named "The Canary." After six months of dedicated training, Amelia achieved a remarkable feat by setting a world altitude record for female pilots, reaching 14,000 feet (about 4,267 meters) in her Airster.

On May 16, 1923, Amelia Earhart earned her pilot's license, becoming the 16th woman in the United States to achieve this honor. Her journey from curious spectator to accomplished pilot was filled with determination, courage, and a deep love for the freedom of the skies.

Overcoming Financial Obstacles

Amelia Earhart's dreams of flying faced a serious setback in the early 1920s due to financial difficulties.

After a failed investment in a gypsum mine, Amelia's inheritance from her grandmother, which her mother managed, began to dwindle. With her flying prospects uncertain, Amelia made the difficult decision to sell her beloved airplanes—the "Canary" and another Kinner—to support herself. She used the money to purchase a striking yellow Kissel Gold Bug "Speedster" automobile, affectionately named the "Yellow Peril."

Despite her efforts to change direction and explore new ventures, Amelia's health issues persisted. Her sinus problems became increasingly painful, leading to another unsuccessful operation in early 1924, which left her frustrated and discouraged.

Amelia didn't give up. She tried various business ventures, including starting a photography company, but none provided the fulfillment she sought.

Charting New Paths

Amelia Earhart faced significant changes and challenges in the wake of her parents' divorce in 1924, but she continued to forge her own path with determination and resilience.

After her parents' divorce, Amelia embarked on an epic transcontinental journey with her mother in their iconic "Yellow Peril" automobile. They traveled from California, making stops across the western United States and venturing up to Banff, Alberta, before finally arriving in Boston, Massachusetts. During this time, Amelia underwent a successful sinus operation, which brought her relief from her chronic health issues.

Following her recovery, Amelia returned to Columbia University for a brief period. However, financial constraints forced her to abandon her studies and her dream of enrolling at the Massachusetts Institute of Technology. Despite these setbacks, Amelia persevered and found employment first as a teacher and later as a social worker at Denison House, a settlement house in Boston.

Even amid her new responsibilities, Amelia's passion for aviation remained strong. She joined the American Aeronautical Society's Boston chapter and became its vice president. She flew regularly from Dennison Airport (later Naval Air Station Squantum) in Quincy, Massachusetts, and even helped finance the airport's operations with her investments.

Amelia's dedication to aviation extended beyond flying. She worked as a sales representative for Kinner Aircraft and wrote newspaper columns promoting aviation and encouraging others to take flight. As her reputation grew, Amelia envisioned an organization dedicated to supporting female aviators.

Flying into History

Amelia Earhart's daring spirit soared to new heights in 1928 after Charles Lindbergh's historic solo flight across the Atlantic Ocean inspired a wave of aviation dreams.

Following Lindbergh's accomplishment, Amy Guest wanted to sponsor the first woman to fly across the Atlantic. Although she deemed the journey too dangerous for herself, Amy Guest sought out another woman with the right image to take on the challenge.

One fateful afternoon in April 1928, Captain Hilton H. Railey called Amelia with a life-changing offer. "Would you like to fly the Atlantic?" he asked. Amelia's heart leaped with excitement as she considered this incredible opportunity.

With project coordinators, including book publisher and publicist George P. Putnam, Amelia was interviewed for the historic flight. She was asked to accompany pilot Wilmer Stultz and co-pilot/mechanic Louis Gordon on the journey and was tasked with keeping the flight log.

On June 17, 1928, the team departed from Trepassey Harbor, Newfoundland, in a Fokker F.VIIb/3m named "Friendship." Amelia, officially a passenger, embarked on an unforgettable 20-hour and 40-minute journey that would make history.

The flight was challenging, with most of it conducted on instruments, and Amelia had no training for this type of flying. She humbly remarked after landing, "Stultz did all the flying—had to. I was just baggage, like a sack of potatoes." Despite this, Amelia's determination shone through as she expressed the desire to fly solo someday.

Amelia's transatlantic adventure didn't end there. On June 19, 1928, she flew an Avro Avian 594 Avian III owned by Irish aviator Lady Mary Heath. This historic flight marked Amelia's strong commitment to aviation, leading her to purchase the aircraft and ship it back to the United States.

Upon returning to the United States on July 6, 1928, Amelia and her crew received a hero's welcome. They were greeted with a ticker-tape parade in Manhattan's Canyon of

Heroes and were honored with a reception at the White House with President Calvin Coolidge.

The Rise of "Lady Lindy"

Amelia Earhart's return to the United States after her historic transatlantic flight catapulted her into the spotlight, earning her the nickname "Lady Lindy" due to her physical resemblance to Charles Lindbergh, the famed aviator known as "Lucky Lindy."

Newspapers and magazines embraced Amelia's growing fame, with some dubbing her "Lady Lindy" and the United Press heralding her as the "Queen of the Air." Amelia's remarkable achievements and charismatic presence captivated the public imagination.

Following her return, Amelia embarked on an exhausting lecture tour throughout 1928 and 1929, sharing her experiences and inspiring audiences across the country. Meanwhile, her publisher and publicist, George P. Putnam, launched an ambitious marketing campaign to promote Amelia and capitalize on her newfound celebrity.

As part of the campaign, Amelia authored a book and embarked on new lecture tours. Her image appeared in mass-market endorsements for products ranging from luggage to women's clothing and sportswear, including an unfortunate association with Lucky Strike cigarettes that caused some image concerns.

Despite challenges, the marketing campaign succeeded in cementing the "Earhart mystique" in the public's mind. Amelia actively engaged in promoting women's fashions, advocating for simple, natural lines matched with practical materials—reflecting her own sleek, purposeful, yet feminine style.

Amelia's influence extended beyond aviation, as she lent her name to a range of promotional items, including the Modernaire Earhart Luggage line. Each item bearing the Earhart name became a symbol of adventure and independence.

Through her endorsements and fashion statements, Amelia Earhart emerged not only as a pioneering aviator but also as a cultural icon—an embodiment of courage, style, and determination.

Advocacy and Achievements

Amelia Earhart's fame and strategic endorsements not only propelled her aviation career but also enabled her to advocate for greater opportunities for women in aviation.

Celebrity endorsements played a crucial role in financing Amelia's flying pursuits. She accepted a position as associate editor at Cosmopolitan magazine, leveraging this platform to champion the acceptance of aviation in society, particularly highlighting the importance of women in the field.

In 1929, Amelia was appointed by Transcontinental Air Transport (TAT, later

TWA) to promote air travel, with a special emphasis on encouraging women to embrace aviation. She invested her time and resources in establishing the Ludington Airline, the first regional shuttle service between New York and Washington, DC.

Amelia's impact extended beyond promotions. She held the role of Vice President of National Airways, overseeing flying operations for Boston-Maine Airways and other airlines in the northeast. Over time, National Airways evolved into Northeast Airlines by 1940.

In 1934, Amelia used her influence to support Isabel Ebel, advocating for her acceptance as the first woman student of Aeronautical Engineering at NYU. This act demonstrated Amelia's commitment to paving the way for women in traditionally male-dominated fields.

Breaking Barriers and Setting Records

Amelia Earhart, determined to carve her own path in aviation, pursued ambitious records and achievements beyond her transatlantic fame.

Shortly after her return from the transatlantic flight, Amelia embarked on her first long solo flight in August 1928. Piloting Avian 7083, she made history by becoming the first woman to fly solo across the North American continent and back. This feat marked a significant milestone in Amelia's aviation career, showcasing her growing piloting skills and professionalism.

Amelia's talents caught the attention of experienced pilots like General Leigh Wade, who praised her as a "born flier" with a delicate touch on the controls.

In 1929, Amelia entered her first competitive air race, the Santa Monica-to-Cleveland Women's Air Derby, affectionately dubbed the "Powder Puff Derby" by Will Rogers. During the race, Amelia settled into fourth place in the "heavy planes" division. The race took a dramatic turn when her friend Ruth Nichols suffered an accident during a test flight, altering the race's outcome.

Amelia's passion for aviation extended beyond racing. In 1930, she became an official of the National Aeronautic Association, advocating for separate women's records and international standards recognized by the Fédération Aéronautique Internationale (FAI).

On April 8, 1931, Amelia set a world altitude record of 18,415 feet (5,613 m) flying a Pitcairn PCA-2 autogyro borrowed from Beech-Nut Chewing Gum. This achievement further solidified her place in aviation history.

During this period, Amelia was instrumental in founding The Ninety-Nines, an organization of female pilots dedicated to providing support and advancing women in aviation. Amelia's leadership and advocacy paved the way for greater opportunities for women in the skies.

A Unique Partnership

Amelia Earhart's personal life took an unconventional turn when she became engaged to Samuel Chapman, a chemical engineer from Boston. However, she broke off the engagement in November 1928.

Around the same time, Amelia grew closer to her publisher, George P. Putnam, known as GP. Putnam was divorced in 1929 and pursued Amelia persistently, proposing to her six times before she agreed to marry him. They tied the knot on February 7, 1931, at Putnam's mother's house in Noank, Connecticut.

Amelia viewed her marriage to Putnam as a "partnership" with "dual control."

Amelia's views on marriage were progressive for her time. She believed in equal responsibilities for both partners and retained her own name, preferring not to be referred to as "Mrs. Putnam." This choice challenged traditional gender roles, reflecting Amelia's independent spirit.

Despite their deep connection, Amelia and Putnam did not have children together. Putnam had two sons from his previous marriage to Dorothy Binney, an heiress to the Crayola crayons company.

Amelia's marriage to George P. Putnam marked a significant chapter in her life, characterized by mutual respect and a shared commitment to independence and adventure.

Breaking Barriers Across Continents

On May 20, 1932, at the age of 34, Amelia Earhart embarked on a daring solo flight from Harbour Grace, Newfoundland, aiming to replicate Charles Lindbergh's legendary solo flight across the Atlantic five years earlier.

Equipped with a copy of the Telegraph-Journal as proof of the flight's date, Amelia set off in her single-engine Lockheed Vega 5B bound for Paris. Her technical advisor, Bernt Balchen, meticulously prepared her aircraft for the challenging journey. Balchen also cleverly acted as a "decoy" for the press, pretending to prepare the Vega for his own Arctic flight.

Amelia faced formidable obstacles during her 14-hour, 56-minute flight, contending with strong, northerly winds, icy conditions, and mechanical issues. Despite these challenges, she successfully touched down in a pasture at Culmore, north of Derry, Northern Ireland. When asked by a farmhand if she had flown far, Amelia famously replied, "From America."

As the first woman to complete a solo nonstop transatlantic flight, Amelia Earhart received prestigious accolades for her achievement. Congress awarded her the Distinguished Flying Cross, the French Government honored her with the Cross of Knight of the Legion of Honor, and President Herbert Hoover presented her with the

Gold Medal of the National Geographic Society.

Amelia's remarkable feat catapulted her to even greater fame and opened doors to new friendships and opportunities. She developed a close bond with First Lady Eleanor Roosevelt, who shared Amelia's passion for women's causes. Although Roosevelt briefly explored the idea of learning to fly after flying with Amelia, she ultimately did not pursue it.

During this period, Amelia also formed a friendship with Jacqueline Cochran, another accomplished aviator often regarded as her rival. Despite their competitive reputation, Cochran became Amelia's trusted confidante, highlighting the camaraderie among pioneering women in aviation.

Setting Records and New Horizons

In January 1935, Amelia Earhart achieved another remarkable feat by becoming the first aviator to fly solo from Honolulu, Hawaii, to Oakland, California. She embarked on this daring journey aboard a Lockheed 5C Vega, making history as she navigated across the vast Pacific Ocean. Despite the challenges of a transoceanic flight, Earhart's voyage was remarkably smooth, with no major mechanical issues. In her final hours of the flight, she even relaxed by listening to the broadcast of the Metropolitan Opera from New York.

Later that year, Earhart once again took to the skies in her trusted Lockheed Vega, affectionately nicknamed "Old Bessie, the fire horse," for a solo flight from Los Angeles to Mexico City on April 19. Undeterred by the distance, she then attempted a nonstop flight from Mexico City to New York on May 8. Upon arrival in Newark, New Jersey, Earhart was greeted by enthusiastic crowds, requiring careful navigation to avoid taxiing into the throng.

Earhart's passion for air racing continued as she participated in the 1935 Bendix Trophy Race, where she secured a respectable fifth-place finish. Despite her skill and determination, her stock Lockheed Vega, capable of reaching speeds up to 195 mph, faced fierce competition from purpose-built air racers exceeding 300 mph. This race was particularly challenging, marked by tragedy, as a competitor lost his life in a fiery mishap during takeoff.

Between 1930 and 1935, Earhart set an impressive seven women's speed and distance aviation records, flying various aircraft, including the Kinner Airster, Lockheed Vega, and Pitcairn Autogiro. By 1935, she recognized the limitations of her beloved Lockheed Vega for long transoceanic flights and began contemplating her next ambitious goal—a circumnavigation of the globe along its equator. This dream required a new aircraft, setting the stage for Amelia Earhart's next groundbreaking adventure.

MARK LYLANI

Flight Ventures in California

While Amelia Earhart was on a speaking tour in late November 1934, a fire devastated the Putnam residence in Rye, destroying cherished family heirlooms and Earhart's personal belongings. This event prompted Amelia and her husband, George P. Putnam, to make a significant decision—they would relocate to the West Coast. Putnam had sold his interest in a New York-based publishing company to his cousin, Palmer Putnam, and took on a new role as head of the editorial board at Paramount Pictures in North Hollywood.

During her time in California, Earhart connected with Hollywood stunt pilot Paul

Mantz to enhance her flying skills, especially in long-distance flights with her trusted Vega aircraft. In June 1935, Putnam purchased a small house adjacent to the Lakeside Golf Club in Toluca Lake, a prestigious community nestled between Warner Brothers and Universal Pictures studios. Although they delayed moving in due to remodeling, the new residence would become their home for the next chapter of their lives.

In September 1935, Earhart and Mantz solidified their partnership by establishing the Earhart-Mantz Flying School at Burbank Airport, just five miles from their Toluca Lake home. Mantz, through his aviation company, United Air Services, operated the school, which focused on teaching instrument flying using Link Trainers. Meanwhile, Putnam took charge of publicity for the school, showcasing Amelia's commitment to advancing aviation education.

Amelia Earhart's influence extended beyond her flying ventures. In 1935, she joined Purdue University as a visiting faculty member, counseling women on career opportunities and serving as a technical advisor to the Department of Aeronautics. Amelia's move to California marked a new phase in her aviation journey, blending Hollywood connections with her passion for flying and education.

MARK LYLANI

Planning the Record-Breaking Flight

In early 1936, Amelia Earhart embarked on an ambitious plan to circumnavigate the globe, aiming to set a new record for the longest flight ever completed. With financial support from Purdue University, Earhart collaborated with Lockheed Aircraft Company to design and build a special aircraft for this daring mission.

The aircraft, a Lockheed Electra 10E (registration NR16020), was customized to Earhart's specifications. It underwent extensive modifications, particularly to the fuselage, which incorporated multiple additional fuel tanks to maximize the plane's range. Earhart affectionately dubbed this twin-engine monoplane her "flying laboratory," as it would serve as both her mode of transportation and a platform for her endeavors.

Captain Harry Manning, an experienced navigator and pilot whom Earhart had previously sailed with on the President Roosevelt, was selected to accompany her on the journey. Manning possessed exceptional skills in navigation and radio operation, making him an invaluable asset for the expedition.

Initially planned as a two-person crew, Earhart and Manning would handle the flight across the vast oceans and challenging terrains. However, concerns arose about Manning's navigation skills during a test flight, prompting the search for an additional navigator.

Enter Fred Noonan, a seasoned navigator with extensive experience in both marine and flight navigation. Noonan had played a crucial role in establishing Pan Am's Pacific routes and training its navigators. His expertise made him an ideal candidate to join Earhart's team, particularly for the challenging leg from Hawaii to Howland Island.

The Lockheed Electra was equipped with specialized radio equipment, including a modified transmitter and receiver designed to communicate on specific frequencies essential for navigation and communication during the flight. Despite some technical challenges with the radio direction finder equipment, Earhart and her team continued to prepare diligently for their historic journey.

With her aircraft ready and her crew assembled, Amelia Earhart was on the brink of embarking on a record-breaking adventure that would captivate the world and etch her name in aviation history.

The Mystery of Howland Island

On March 17, 1937, Amelia Earhart embarked on her round-the-world flight once more, this time with renewed determination. The first leg of her journey from Oakland, California, to Honolulu, Hawaii, commenced smoothly, with Earhart joined by Fred Noonan and Harry Manning aboard her specially modified Lockheed Electra 10E. Their mission was to circumnavigate the globe, setting records and inspiring millions.

However, their plans were soon marred by mechanical issues. Problems with the propeller hubs forced an unplanned stop at the United States Navy's Luke Field in Pearl Harbor. After a brief delay for repairs, Earhart and her crew resumed their journey towards Howland Island.

The flight from Luke Field was fraught with challenges from the start. During takeoff, disaster struck as the aircraft veered off course in an uncontrolled ground loop. The landing gear collapsed, propellers hit the ground, and the plane skidded to a halt. The cause of this harrowing crash remains uncertain, with witnesses offering conflicting accounts.

With the Electra severely damaged, Earhart's ambitious attempt was abruptly halted. The aircraft was shipped back to Lockheed Burbank in California for extensive repairs, marking a setback in their quest to make history.

Undeterred by this setback, Amelia Earhart and George Putnam persisted. They secured additional funds and meticulously planned a second attempt, this time flying west to east. Departing from Oakland on an unpublicized flight to Miami, Florida, Earhart publicly announced her intentions to circumnavigate the globe once more.

For the second attempt, Manning departed from the crew, leaving only Noonan and Earhart to navigate the arduous journey ahead. Their route took them across continents, stopping in South America, Africa, and Asia before arriving at Lae, New Guinea, on June 29, 1937.

With over 22,000 miles (about 35,405 kilometers) behind them, Earhart and Noonan prepared for the most daunting leg of their journey—an ambitious flight over the vast expanse of the Pacific Ocean to

Howland Island. The journey was a test of endurance and navigation skills, with the destination lying 2,556 miles (about 4,113 kilometers) away from Lae.

The US Coast Guard stationed the USCGC Itasca at Howland Island to provide vital communication and navigation support. As Earhart and Noonan approached their destination on July 2, 1937, they encountered numerous challenges. Despite strong radio transmissions from Earhart, she struggled to receive signals from the Itasca due to technical issues with the direction-finding equipment.

With fuel running low and time slipping away, Earhart's final transmissions indicated confusion and desperation. The world anxiously awaited news of their arrival, but the once-clear signals grew faint, leaving a sense of uncertainty and mystery.

Amidst a flurry of conflicting reports and hoaxes, the fate of Amelia Earhart and Fred Noonan remained shrouded in uncertainty. Despite exhaustive search efforts, their disappearance marked a tragic end to a courageous journey that captured the world's imagination and left behind an enduring legacy of bravery and exploration.

The Search for Answers

The US government wanted to find out what happened to Amelia Earhart, so they looked into her disappearance. They thought that her plane had run out of fuel and crashed into the ocean. In the 1970s, a retired Navy captain named Laurance Safford studied the flight in detail. He looked at all the radio messages and decided that the flight wasn't planned or executed very well.

Many people believe that Amelia Earhart and Fred Noonan died in the crash or shortly after. In 1982, another retired Navy admiral named Richard R. Black, who was at Howland Island when Earhart disappeared, said that he thought the plane went into the ocean around 10 a.m. on July 2, 1937, not far from the island. Amelia Earhart's stepson, George Palmer Putnam Jr., thought that the plane ran out of fuel.

Some researchers think that Earhart's plane is on the seafloor, about 17,000 feet (5 kilometers) below the surface. Others believe it's even deeper, at 18,000 feet. British aviation historian Roy Nesbit looked at old accounts and letters and said he didn't think the plane had been fully fueled before it took off from Lae.

There have been many search efforts over the years to find Earhart's plane. In 2024, a company called Deep Sea Vision found what they think might be her plane using special underwater vehicles and sonar. The object they found looks like Earhart's plane, and it's deep underwater, not far from Howland

Island. Now, they need to do more exploring to be sure if this is really Amelia Earhart's missing aircraft.

Theories and Speculations

While many believe that Amelia Earhart's disappearance was simply due to a crash and sinking of her aircraft into the ocean, there are numerous other theories and conspiracy ideas that have captured people's imaginations.

One theory suggests that Amelia and her navigator Fred Noonan survived the crash but ended up landing elsewhere, either on a remote island like Gardner Island (now Nikumaroro), which is about 400 miles (640 km) away from Howland Island, or even in Japanese-controlled territories like the Marshall Islands or the Northern Mariana

Islands, which are significantly farther away.

The Gardner Island theory speculates that if they had been unable to locate Howland Island, Amelia and Fred might have turned south in search of other lands. Gardner Island has been a focus of investigation, but no concrete evidence linking Amelia to the island has been discovered.

Another intriguing idea is the Japanese capture theory, which suggests that Amelia and Fred were captured by Japanese forces, possibly after straying into the Japanese South Seas Mandate. Some of Amelia's relatives strongly believed that the Japanese were involved in her disappearance, pointing to unidentified witnesses, including Japanese troops and Saipan natives. One cousin even claimed that the Japanese dismantled Amelia's plane and disposed of it in the ocean to hide evidence.

There's also the New Britain theory, which proposes that Amelia turned back during her flight and attempted to reach the airfield at Rabaul in New Britain, northeast of Papua New Guinea, a staggering 2,200 miles (3,500 km) from Howland Island.

In 1990, an Australian Army veteran named Donald Angwin claimed to have seen a wrecked aircraft in the New Britain jungle in 1945 that he suspected might have been Amelia's Electra. Despite detailed maps and serial numbers, subsequent searches of the area failed to find any wreckage.

A more sensational theory emerged in 1970 with the book "Amelia Earhart Lives," which suggested that Amelia had survived her flight, moved to New Jersey, changed her name to Irene Craigmile Bolam, and even remarried. This claim was based on research by Major Joseph Gervais. However, Irene Bolam denied being Amelia Earhart and even filed a lawsuit against the book's publisher. Detailed studies by forensic experts later confirmed that Irene Bolam was not Amelia Earhart.

A Lasting Legacy in Aviation

Countless tributes and memorials continue to honor Amelia Earhart's remarkable legacy and achievements in aviation.

In 2012, US Secretary of State Hillary Clinton paid tribute to Earhart at a State Department event, highlighting her inspirational impact on anyone who dreams of reaching for the stars.

Flying magazine recognized Earhart as one of the "51 Heroes of Aviation," ranking her at No. 9 in 2013.

During her lifetime, Amelia Earhart was an international celebrity known for her charisma, independence, and courage. Her story continues to captivate popular culture, inspiring hundreds of articles and numerous books. Earhart's life is often celebrated as a motivational tale, particularly encouraging for girls, and she is widely regarded as a feminist icon.

Earhart's accomplishments paved the way for future female aviators. Over 1,000 women pilots of the Women Airforce Service Pilots (WASP) were inspired by Earhart's example to serve in various capacities during World War II.

Amelia Earhart's birthplace in Atchison, Kansas, is now the Amelia Earhart Birthplace Museum, maintained by The Ninety-Nines, an international group of female pilots. The town also hosts the annual Amelia Earhart Festival since 1996.

Purdue University, where Earhart was a career counselor and technical advisor, honors her with Earhart Hall, a bronze statue, and plans for the Amelia Earhart Terminal at the Purdue University Airport.

Statues and monuments across the United States commemorate Earhart's legacy, including a bronze statue at the Spirit of Flight Center in Lafayette, Colorado, and one in Los Angeles, California.

Amelia Earhart's name is immortalized in various ways: a Liberty ship named SS Amelia Earhart, USNS Amelia Earhart, Amelia Earhart Airport in Atchison, Kansas, and a commemorative stamp issued in 1963 by the United States Postmaster-General.

Earhart's impact extends beyond aviation. She was inducted into the Motorsports Hall of Fame of America in 1992, and landmarks like the Amelia Earhart Dam in Massachusetts and the "Earhart Tree" in Hilo, Hawaii, planted by Earhart herself in 1935, also honor her memory.

In 1967, Ann Dearing Holtgren Pellegreno retraced Earhart's flight plan in a Lockheed 10A Electra, dropping a wreath over Howland Island on the 30th anniversary of Earhart's disappearance.

Linda Finch replicated Earhart's final flight path in 1997 using a restored 1935 Lockheed Electra 10E, and in 2001, Dr. Carlene Mendieta retraced Earhart's 1928 transcontinental record flight in an original Avro Avian.

Amelia Earhart's legacy continues to inspire generations of aviators and dreamers, leaving an indelible mark on history and the pursuit of dreams.

MARK LYLANI

CONCLUSION

As we conclude this journey through the remarkable life of Amelia Earhart, we reflect on the indelible mark she left on the world of aviation and beyond. Amelia's story is not just one of daring flights and record-breaking achievements but also resilience, passion, and unwavering determination.

Throughout her life, Amelia faced numerous challenges and obstacles, from financial constraints to societal barriers, yet she never allowed these hurdles to ground her dreams. Instead, she soared above them, charting new paths and inspiring countless individuals to reach for the skies.

Amelia's legacy extends far beyond her disappearance on that fateful flight over the Pacific. She continues to inspire adventurers, aviators, and dreamers of all ages to push boundaries, break barriers, and embrace the spirit of exploration.

As we look back on Amelia Earhart's extraordinary life, may we remember her as more than a historical figure; may we carry forward her spirit of courage and determination, ensuring that her legacy of exploration and empowerment lives on for generations to come.

In Amelia's words, "Adventure is worthwhile in itself." Let us continue to embark on our own adventures, guided by the fearless example set by this trailblazing aviator.